The Bad Back Book

THE BAD BACK BOOK

Jerry Wayne

OX BOW PRESS
Woodbridge, Connecticut

Ox Bow Press
P.O. Box 4045
Woodbridge, CT 06525
(203) 387-5900

Manufactured in the United States of America

Ox Bow Press, reprint — 1983

Library of Congress Cataloging in Publication Data

Wayne, Jerry
The bad back book.

Autobiographical.
1. Intervertebral disc displacement—Personal narratives. 2. Gymnastics, Medical. I. Title. RD771.16W39 617'.37 [B] 82-062473

ISBN — 0-918024-25-0

An open letter from Eugene B. Levin, M.D.

I am constantly hearing doctors discuss the problem of treating patients with back trouble. We all seem to prescribe much the same remedies —pain-killers, diathermy, bed rest, traction and, finally, surgery—and up until now that was all we could do. But now there is *The Bad Back Book*, and I believe this series of exercises will bring as much relief to overworked doctors as to desperate patients. For these exercises *work*.

Of course there are certain extreme cases where exercises may not be indicated and in these cases a go-ahead from your doctor is advisable.

I have frequently suggested to my patients that they should "get more exercise." Now, for millions of back sufferers like himself, Jerry Wayne has collected exercises from various countries of Europe and Asia and laid down a program which is easy to follow and which produces amazing results. If these exercises are carried out regularly, back pain can be permanently eliminated.

The Bad Back Book shows you how to strengthen your back. If your back is strong, you will not have backaches. It really is as simple as that.

I intend to prescribe *The Bad Back Book* in very liberal doses.

Because it works!

TO DOREEN,
whose invaluable help
almost gave her a bad back

And a special "thank you" to
Martin H. Waldman

The Bad Back Book

IN 1951 I was starring in the Broadway musical *Finian's Rainbow*. Each evening I made my first entrance from behind a rock. Each evening I delivered my opening line and waited for the laugh. Each evening I made a five-foot leap onto the stage below me . . . and one evening I failed to get up.

For the first five minutes the audience thought my all-fours crouch was part of the show, and although they may not have found it particularly entertaining, they were prepared to wait for better things to come. My co-actors, similarly, were hoping for better things, thinking perhaps that the long delay in my getting up and speaking line two were part of the Method school of acting and therefore to be tolerated. However, anxious, silent minutes ticked by and there I remained, frozen to the spot. For I was paralyzed. No matter how I struggled and strained, I couldn't move one muscle in my entire body. Only my sweat glands were active, dropping puddles onto the stage as the patience of the audience finally wore out and a restless muttering filled the crowded theater. I prayed for something to happen, anything, and it did—an agonizing flash of pain streaked from my back along my right leg. And then I was paralyzed *and* in agony, suffering too much to think of a way of signaling to the other actors that something had gone terribly wrong. They assumed I'd "dried up," forgotten the opening lines, and like real old pros they began to throw ad-libs while the prompter hissed my line loudly enough for the balcony to hear. Coughing, shuffling and mumbling came from the audience and then a loud, lone, shrill giggle, which sent the lightning pain flashing worse than ever. And at last the stage manager realized something was wrong. He brought down the fire curtain, missing my head by inches, and the stagehands surrounded me in a hissing, whispering circle. I still couldn't speak or move and finally they lifted me bodily and carried me away, still in a crouch position. And as I went I could hear the stage manager yelling, "Everybody hold your places—we'll make an announcement. Get the understudy ready, for God's sake!"

I was taken to my dressing room and, still in excruciating pain, dumped unceremoniously on the bed while everybody rushed out to ensure that the show would go on. And finally the company manager staggered in.

"Don't move," he instructed, somewhat needlessly I thought, "there's a doctor coming." And he was gone, leaving me alone to sort out my popcorn-machine thoughts, each colliding numbly with the others until one came to the surface. Would I ever play tennis again? Tennis? Tennis! Would I ever *walk* again? Was I paralyzed? Had I broken my neck/back/spine/. . . contract? No, not my contract—it didn't say I couldn't collapse on stage and ruin the performance . . . but it did say that I could only be out sick for a few days. The pain I was experiencing was so intense, so overwhelming, that I couldn't imagine *ever* recovering from it, much less in a few days. And while I lay there in the dog-paddle position, wondering numbly what was taking the doctor so long, I passed out.

Dr. W. said, "How d'ya feel, Mr. Wayne?" as though he didn't care at all and I wondered if he'd had tickets to that performance.

"Try moving," he suggested, now slightly warmer. Perhaps he'd realized that a professional visit would permit him to deduct the $10 from his taxes. "Take it easy. I just gave you a shot to relieve the spasm but I don't know what damage there is. *Easy*, okay?"

Cautiously I tried to move and found I was able to. A burning pain flashed from my back down the right leg, but I was moving and, with a little help from the doctor, even sitting up. A stream of chorus people and actors stuck their heads around the door as they awaited their next entrance and I tried to smile at them, but the pain, plus the sound of my understudy's voice working over "Old Devil Moon" soon wiped the smile off my face. "Hey, Doc, how am I going to get home?" I asked anxiously.

"Try getting up," he suggested, lending a hand—and immediately the pain hit me like a fist.

"We'll carry you to a cab," the doctor said, beckoning to a couple of beefy stagehands and quickly stepping back.

"What about at the other end?" I yelled and my bearers stopped, jarring me badly.

"Can't your wife help you out?" Dr. W. inquired and I wondered if he thought I was married to a couple of stagehands. Big ones.

"Maybe the cabdriver will help," I muttered and the doctor nodded quickly and left. My bearers started up again and, helped along by good wishes and friendly pats (painful ones) from the backstage crew and cast, we struggled into a taxi.

I'd forgotten how small my wife was. And since receiving the stage manager's phone call about my whatever-it-was, she'd shrunk another few inches from worry. Anyway, she was obviously going to be as much help as a three-legged ant and I turned to the cabdriver with my best let-'em-see-your-teeth-at-the-back-of-the-house smile.

"I gotta get back to Manhattan, buddy," he complained. Not a theatergoer, obviously.

Well, I spent the next ten minutes trying to sit up while my wife stuck her hand through the door to help and knocked me down again, and the driver told me that the meter was ticking. He mentioned that several times, in fact. I suspect it was only my assurance that I was a man of independent means—independently poor, that is—that stopped him from driving off with me half in and half out of the cab like a big hamburger in a small bun. Anyway, with great charm and forbearance and only a small amount of spitting and cursing, the driver climbed into the cab with me and, following my instructions carefully, managed to cantilever me out and into the arms of my wife. Then they both maneuvered me up the outside stairs, through the lobby, into the elevator, and up to my fifth-floor apartment. I lay in agony on the bed while my wife tried to beat the cabdriver down to only half my month's pay and finally, muttering something about "rotten actors," he stumped away. I hoped he didn't mean professionally. I was in no mood for a critique.

My wife immediately called our doctor while I tried to find a comfortable position, but each time I moved, the pain radiated down my leg and finally I lay still, just giving up. Then my wife informed me that our doctor wouldn't make a house call; I had to visit his office the next day and, man, did I move then. Churning onto my side, bellowing with pain, I roared obscenities about the medical profession which, literally, hurt me more than they did him. Finally, after being forced to admit that our apartment did not have X-ray, infra-red, or any other equipment outside of a toaster, I agreed to make the trip—on condition I lived. Dr. G. promised I would and hedged his bet by prescribing some pain-killers.

Shortly after I'd taken them I was sound asleep and dreaming fitfully that I was a football player with all the men on the field, my side included, kicking me in the back. And I woke up thinking, "Whoever heard of an actor being sent off with a back injury," which thought grew even more amusing when I realized that I felt pretty good. The muscle spasms had subsided and I could move freely without apparent pain. For a moment I wondered if the whole thing had been a dream, but then the horror of being struck down in front of a paying audience returned to haunt me and I knew I hadn't imagined it at all.

My wife was in the bathroom and I decided I would be nonchalantly strolling around the living room when she finally emerged. I swung my legs over the bed—no problem moving, no pain. I stood up—and almost fell down again. The moment I put pressure on my legs, the sharp pain returned and shot down my right leg. I hobbled into the living room and flopped into a chair, which stopped the shooting pain but left me with the burning sensation in my lower back. My pale, worried wife appeared and I asked her to again request that our doctor visit me at home, but again he refused, insisting that it would hurt me but not harm me to go to his office. And oh, man, did it *hurt*. I lay on his examination table and tried to remember the ride over, but the pain had been so fierce that my mind rejected it and I couldn't recollect any part of it.

Dr. G. tapped various parts of my legs to test the reflexes and generally poked and prodded me while I told him what had happened and then he took X rays and told me to go home. His advice was to take pain-killers, to stay off my feet—preferably in bed—for at least four weeks. Four weeks out of the show! Oh, brother!

Flat on my back in bed was the only place I felt halfway human. There the pain lifted enough for me to worry myself to death about the possibility of getting fired. The show had been running for three years and no longer really needed stars to pull in the public. My Equity contract allowed the producers to replace me if I was unduly absent and put in an actor who got less money—and why shouldn't they, now that they had a big smash? I was so nervous I could hardly wait to call the theater, but they were so nice to me and so concerned about my health that they really did me more good than the pain-killers. And one week later my notice of termination of contract arrived. I called Equity, my agent, my lawyer, my rabbi—anybody who could be of help. Equity said the producers had the right; my agent wouldn't come to the phone; my lawyer demanded I pay my old bill before asking for new advice; and my rabbi recommended prayer. And none of it worked, anyway. I was fired.

Dr. G.'s X rays showed negative. He found absolutely no damage to my spinal column or any small bones around the base of my spine. He found no trace of nerve injury and the muscles all looked in good shape. It was his opinion that the four weeks' rest would fix everything, so who cared about one lousy great show?

Four weeks later I got out of bed, put my weight on my legs, the pain returned exactly as before and I might just as well have never been resting at all. Now Dr. G. recommended traction. This is a medieval torture carried out in the hospital where they attach weights to your legs in an attempt to stretch your spinal column. This is done so that the pinched sciatic nerve, which is what causes the pain to travel down your leg, is relieved of any pressure. Dr. G. assured me that two weeks of this treatment would make all the difference and again assured me that I would live.

He was right. I lived. And after two weeks of agony

the pain *was* different. It was worse. Now I was half out of my mind, but Dr. G., still very calm and cool, recommended I see a specialist, Dr. Alice F., who had offices on Park Avenue. She practiced a modern variation of the six-thousand-year-old Chinese treatment-for-everything called acupuncture, the inserting of long dry needles into the muscles around the painful area. This specialist called it "her specialty" and charged me $25 for nothing but a back full of holes. Mind you, I'll never forget that visit to Dr. Alice F. It was like a scene from the Marx Brothers. She told me to strip and lie face down on her table and then, as though they were old friends, she greeted every muscle in my back by name. At the same time she jabbed a six-inch needle into each one, which I would have suspected put something of a strain upon the friendship.

"Hello, little gluteus maximus." Jab!

"Erector spinae—how are you?" Bam!

"You can't hide from me, latissimus dorsi." Wham!

At last she had visited with all her friends and turned away from both them and my pin-cushion backside. If I was to escape from this nut, now was the moment. I was up, dressed, and out of that place as fast as supreme agony would permit. And then back to Dr. G. to complain.

"Well, she gets some amazing results," he said judicially.

"I'll bet she does. What now?"

"Maybe a little diathermy, huh?"

I breathed deeply, counted ten, and then explained to the good doctor that I couldn't afford to experiment with every crackpot back treatment ever invented. I was out of work and nearly out of money and wasn't there a recognized specialist who could treat me and get it over with? He said there was a Dr. Ernest W., in New York, who was the top man for top people. At my urging he called for an appointment, then announced sweetly that it was all arranged for five weeks ahead. I nearly leaped through the ceiling and destroyed his thousand-dollar chandelier.

"Five weeks—I'll be out of my mind and out of money by then."

Dr. G. looked anxious. "He charges fifty dollars a visit—are you sure you can afford it?"

"Your concern for my sanity is touching," I snapped. "Fifty dollars! What's he doing, giving away blue-chip stamps?"

"No, just knowledge," Dr. G. said coolly, having known me for several years and heard most of my routines. "If you want the best, you have to pay for it."

So it was five weeks. And I counted every minute in pain and worry.

Dr. Ernest W. tapped the tendons in my legs for reflexes, prodded and poked my back to find painful areas, measured my hamstring and thigh muscles for atrophy, and asked me to walk away from him while he watched for a favoring limp or tilt to one side. Then he examined Dr. G.'s X rays and, nodding knowledgeably, invited me to sit facing him across his desk.

"You have a severe case of sciatica which is caused by pressure on the sciatic nerve. This radiates pain to your ankle where the nerve ends. You may have a slipped disc."

I'd heard the diagnosis and now I waited eagerly for the remedy.

Silence.

"What do I do to get cured, Doctor?" I asked patiently.

"Have you tried bed rest for a prolonged period?"

I nodded.

"No relief, hmm?"

I shook my head.

"Traction?"

I again nodded, this time more slowly.

"No help?"

I shook my head, afraid to believe what I already was believing.

"How much time do you have to try non-drastic measures?"

"Little or none. What do you mean 'non-drastic'? What are the drastic measures?"

"Surgery," he said casually.

"Surgery? Is it that bad?" I asked, stunned.

"It may not be, but if you can't spare the time for more bed rest and diathermy . . ."

He shrugged and I shuddered. "Okay," I said, beaten, "I'll go back to bed. I'm sure not ready for surgery yet."

"Fine," he beamed, "twelve weeks and it must be total rest. Understand? No getting out, even to go to the–er–" He gestured delicately and I got the message. No toilet, no standing, no walking–and no work. I was really desperate. Not only was the thought of so much enforced inactivity anathema to a restless character like me, I'd also miss the August casting for the fall shows, so even when I was cured, twelve weeks later, I'd be out of work for God knows how long. Worried and despondent, I trekked home and called my agent with the good news. He immediately suggested his own remedy for back trouble–a chiropractor–and I exploded wildly against "those phonies." But the name kept recurring as I called my friends for sympathy, and I started to have a re-think. After all, what could be worse than acupuncture or twelve weeks in bed? So, armed with fresh hope and a recommendation from my best friend, Al, I paid a visit to Malcolm Calvin L. (D.C.) on Eighty-sixth Street and Lexington Avenue.

Dr. L. was a small man with large glasses on a pug nose. The glasses kept slipping down and he kept pushing them up, a reasonable attempt at perpetual motion and a battle he was doomed to lose unless he turned to plastic surgery. Instead he turned to me.

"Please undress, Mr. Wayne," he said, smiling.

I did.

"Lie down, please, on your stomach."

I had visions of Dr. Alice F. talking to my ass and wondered what this one was up to. I didn't have long to wait. He put his oak-tree arms under my chest and bent me back until I resembled a pretzel–then I heard a crack.

"Mm. Good," he said happily.

The crack had caused pain to shoot down my leg, but when I yelled, Malcolm Calvin L. just smiled contentedly. Ignoring my pleas and threats, he turned me this way and that, twisting me into weird, painful positions and piling on the agony until he heard that loud crack, the signal for me to groan and him to smile.

Forty minutes later Little Malcolm, sweating, grinning, and pushing at his glasses, told me to rise and walk around. I did, and the pain was about the worst I had experienced so far. While Malcolm optimistically booked me in for a half-dozen new appointments, I struggled into my clothes, jolted home in agony and despair, and collapsed into bed for twelve long, miserable weeks.

I read books, talked to visiting friends, argued with my wife, tried not to develop bedsores, and throughout this hectic activity forced myself not to think about surgery. Everyone who called had apparently had a slipped disc in the family (kept secret before this) and without exception these skeleton-in-the-closet relatives had had to resort to surgery. As I heard it, the operation plus fusion, the new method, worked perfectly and the patients were soon up and about and back to work again. So what was I worrying about? Particularly since I probably wouldn't need surgery anyway, since the bed rest was going to do the trick–right?

The twelve weeks finally ground to an end and the wonderful, exciting, nerve-shattering day for getting up was with me. Watched by my apprehensive wife, who had a bright smile painted grimly on her face, I slowly and carefully moved my legs over the side of the bed. Then, oh so tentatively, I placed them on the floor. Half leaning on my wife's shoulder, I stood up and a wave of dizziness washed over me. My legs felt like overcooked spaghetti and I collapsed onto the bed as weak and helpless as a child. But not in any pain. I rested for a minute or two and tried again. This time I stood for a brief moment, then took a step. My legs were skinny and weak but still no pain had returned. I stood still, walked a few steps, stood still, and walked a few more. I entered the living room and it looked larger than I remembered it. It was so good to be up I was actually wreathed in smiles. I walked slowly and falteringly to the armchair and carefully lowered myself into it. It was amazingly good to be off my feet considering how desperately I wanted to be *on* them.

"Take it easy, honey. You're weak from not exercising. How does it feel?"

"Not bad. No pain," I said, beaming.

"Great," she said, all smiles. "How about a cup of coffee?"

"No thanks. I want to walk a little more."

"Sure?"

"Yeah. Help me up, please."

She half lifted me and I did the rest. This time I walked alone, unaided, from the chair to the kitchen and back again. The legs were feeling more like legs and the dizziness had passed. I headed for the bedroom and suddenly, disbelievingly, I thought I felt a faint twinge of pain in my back. I stopped abruptly.

"What's wrong, sweetheart?" my wife asked anxiously.

"I don't know. I'm not sure. I thought I felt something."

"Get back into bed. You're doing too much for the first time."

I quietly did as she suggested, fell back onto the pillow, and closed my eyes, saying a silent prayer: "If the pain returns now, I'll flip my lid, so help me God."

"Do you want some codeine?"

"No. I've got to know if it worked. Call the doc and ask him how much I can do the first day."

In a minute or two she was back.

"He said not to overdo it. Ten or fifteen minutes at a time until your legs strengthen."

"Ten or fifteen . . . I did about three!"

I threw the covers back and moved my legs over the side. I felt no pain and my legs seemed stronger. I started walking slowly around the apartment. As I reached the window for the third time I suddenly felt the old, unmistakable burning in my back, and when I turned to face the room, the all-too-familiar streak of pain radiated down my right leg. I panicked, rushing out of the room as fast as I could, maybe trying to run away from the pain, while my wife ran alongside me yelling, "What's the matter, what's happened?" By the time I got to the bed I was in as much agony as ever and I struggled to make myself admit the obvious: bed rest had failed. It had all been a tragic waste of time.

I fell back onto the bed, sweating and miserable. If ever I get an acting job where I need to cry I'll just think of that moment and the rest of the cast will be in danger of drowning. Or, talking of casts, I'll think about the next step, which involved sticking me in a plaster cast from neck to hip, immobilizing me for another eight weeks and then discovering that that, too, had failed.

And that's when the decision was made to have surgery.

The surgeon gave me the standard examination, pushing, prodding, reflex testing, muscle measuring, et cetera, and then said I probably had a slipped disc in the lower lumbar region, around the fourth vertebra. He said the one sure way of determining this, bearing my other symptoms in mind, was to take a myelogram which, although temporarily uncomfortable, would only keep me in the hospital overnight. He explained that he would inject a blueish liquid into the fluid layer around the spinal column and then cause the liquid to flow up and down by tilting the examination table back and forth. Apparently, if there were a slipped disc it would prevent the blue liquid from passing freely along the spinal column and a contrast in color would show up on the X ray. I agreed to take part in this fun game in exchange for a little information—like if the test showed a slipped disc, how long after the operation would I be back on the tennis court? The surgeon grinned and said if I'd settle for moving, walking and working (would I!), then he'd say about a month, but it would be a month flat on my back. God—again! It seemed like there was some crazy, fiendish plot afoot to keep me abed—but who was behind it? My understudy was capable of it, but he already had the part!

Anyway, we talked for a while about how I'd be fitted for a back brace and then, after a few months, a surgical corset and eventually, as my back strengthened, I wouldn't need any support and I'd be fit, well and free from pain. It sounded so great that I immediately asked what percentage of failures occurred in this operation. The surgeon hedged, claiming that even taking out tonsils had its failures and I so badly wanted him to fix me up that I didn't press the point. And two days later I went for the myelogram.

Blue has ceased to be my favorite color.

New York General Hospital refused to feed me dinner, denied me even a glass of water (at *their* prices!), woke me from a sound nightmare to take me to the X-ray department, and there injected the blue liquid and began to rock the table. Head up, head down, head up, head down—and I experienced a recurring nausea and dizziness that by comparison made my worst-ever hangover seem like a birthday gift. I thought the torture would never end, but finally I was dumped into my bed and allowed to sleep it off.

Several hours later I awoke to find my wife and a loaded tray beside the bed. I waited for a return of nausea (at sight of the food, of course) but now I felt fine and eagerly tucked into my lunch.

"How was it?" my wife asked.

"It'll never be a hit—I didn't laugh once."

"We'll get our laugh at the results," she said firmly. "They're going to be negative, I just feel it in my bones."

"You can clearly see the obstruction here at lumbar L4," the surgeon said, pointing to the X ray on his view box. "There's no question you have a ruptured slipped disc."

A steel band tightened around my head and I felt my heart beating wildly. I didn't want to burst into tears, so I thought about how I was going to give it to my wife for believing one word her lousy bones said to her. Female intuition? Phooey!

"Surgery, huh?" I asked quietly.

"It certainly seems indicated, since nothing else has helped." He watched me light up two cigarettes at once and said, "Look, there's no great emergency. Why don't you think about it for a little while?"

"No. Once I start thinking I call everything off. I'd stop breathing if I had to think about it. I want you to go ahead, okay?"

The surgeon nodded.

"This minute!"

He smiled. "Will a week from today be soon enough?"

"No. This minute, or not at all. Understand?"

One week later at 8 A.M. I was operated on. At 12:30 my wife swam blearily into view and told me that everything had gone fine and that the surgeon had decided against fusing the vertebrae, so I'd only had the disc removed. A mere bagatelle! She said I'd be up and around in a month, and after checking that this was not intuition but straight from the surgeon's mouth, I allowed myself to fall into a drugged sleep in which I beat Pancho Gonzales 6–0, 6–0, 6–0.

As it turned out, I needed that victory over Pancho

to see me through the four boring weeks in the hospital. Each time I thought about living normally again I was overcome with emotion and had to be given a shot by a large nurse with a mustache and a bad aim. At the end of two weeks my stitches were removed. At the end of the third I was measured for a brace and on D-Day (Departure, that is) the brace was hauled in by the hairy nurse, who seemed the only member of the staff strong enough to lift it. It was a massive, leather-bound iron affair that went from chest to hips and must have weighed fifteen pounds. It took quite a few of them to get it on me, but even on top of that monstrosity my clothes hung as though they belonged to a man half my size . . . which apparently I now was.

I had felt no pain since the operation, and as the surgeon and nurse helped me to stand, I could hardly wait to test my legs.

They failed.

It wasn't pain, but weakness, and I was delighted to flop into a wheelchair and ride out to the waiting taxi. The chair was loaded in beside me, nearly squashing my wife, but she was too drunk with happiness to notice and we rode home hand in hand, hardly speaking but smiling a lot. New York never looked so good to me and I made a resolution on the Triborough Bridge never again to let silly little things bother me. All I asked for was good health and, given it, would live each day to the full, never again complaining about anything. Hmmm!

It was great, great, great to be sitting in my own living room . . . until I noticed that a hospital bed was occupying quite a lot of the remaining space in there.

"What's that contraption for?" I asked suspiciously.

"For you, dear."

"Really? I thought maybe we'd had a child since I was in the hospital. Or a lodger. Or the bailiffs had taken our own stuff. Or . . ."

"I'm so glad you're home!" She beamed.

I relaxed and took hold of her hand.

"Why the bed?" I asked quietly. "I thought after a month I was going to be all cured. Is there something you're not telling me?"

"No. I swear it. The doctor said you should use that bed until you're fully mobile again—it's hard and it can be raised and lowered without jolting you—see?" She demonstrated and I nodded. "You'll be on your feet a little more each day—but you mustn't overdo it. Now that's sensible, isn't it?"

I wanted to argue but couldn't because I was trying to get onto my feet for that day. My wife rushed to help and together we managed maybe two steps before I was thanking God for the hospital bed and longing to be in it.

"Okay, that's enough," my wife instructed and, pretending to be a little unwilling, I collapsed gratefully into bed.

As the days passed I walked more and more and spent

more time out of bed. My strength was returning and I was able, with the brace and a heavy cane, to get around alone. At the end of the first week, Dr. G. suggested I go outside and get some fresh air. The idea of going down the elevator and the front stairs loomed as a great, dangerous expedition, but I wasn't going to look chicken in front of him so I nodded and headed for the door.

I managed the elevator all right, but the stairs were a more difficult proposition. The various levels shifted my body weight and caused my spine to tilt first to one side and then the other. By the third step I was feeling pain in my back, but I dismissed it, attributing it to the postoperative pain which the surgeon had told me I should expect. By the time I got down the steps and wanted to go back up again, I was feeling very much worse and when I finally got back into bed I was in severe pain, although it hadn't radiated down my leg like before the operation. I called the surgeon, who said this reaction was to be expected and advised me to stay in bed for a few days. I was so relieved at the idea of resting that I could have kissed him. I could have kissed Dracula. I was sure relieved!

The days passed, I was again in and out of bed, and I came to accept the constant pain as a temporary way of life. But as the days turned to weeks, my strength had returned and the pain still remained, I began to question the totality of my cure. The surgeon had examined me several times and said he was satisfied with my progress and urged me to be patient. Since I had no other choice, I agreed to try.

A month later the pain had again started radiating down my leg and as far as I could tell I was no better off than before I went in for surgery. Clearly a major decision had to be made about my future. Either I stocked up on pain-killers and tried to go back to work, hoping that time would heal what the medical profession clearly could not, or I would allow myself to become an invalid, letting my wife take care of me until we ran out of money and starved to death on our hospital bed.

It was a tough choice, but eventually I made it.

My agent was delighted to hear that I was ready to go back to work and said I was just in time to audition for the producers of *Guys and Dolls* who were putting together a London company. The idea of going to Europe was a real shot in the arm, the idea of starring in such a great show excited me . . . and at the back of my mind was something better than all of that. I had read that in Europe and Asia they were using new methods for treating back problems that were getting terrific results without surgery. And if I'd needed any more incentive than that to go to an audition, I'd have been nothing less than evil-minded.

I arrived in London on May 13, 1953, in good time for

the coronation of Princess Elizabeth, assuming they decided to invite me. The weather was cold and damp and played havoc with my back, but rehearsals were going great. I was so involved with them, plus discovering London, that most of the time I managed to live with the pain and to function more or less normally. However, there was one scene in the first act of the show that clearly spelled trouble for me. Sky Masterson, the character I played, had to hoist Sarah, the Mission Doll, over his shoulder and carry her out of a nightclub set and into the wings, all at a very fast pace. This particular Mission Doll was a pretty hearty eater and I knew that the agony I was suffering wasn't doing my back any good at all. Unfortunately the action was very important to the scene and got one of the biggest hands in the show. Like the incredibly brave, terrified-of-being-fired hero that I am, I kept quiet until after our tryout in Bristol and the opening in London. After that I confided in the director, and after giving me a big dose of sympathy (he was a back sufferer himself), he allowed me to take Sarah by the hand and drag her off the stage for the rest of our long, successful run. And not one customer asked for his money back.

As the cold winter turned into a beautiful spring, the fancy of this young man turned to . . . tennis, what else? I hadn't been on a court in two years, but I thought about it at least once each day and couldn't pass a court without cursing the players as though they had done me a personal injury by being out there with racket, ball, net, and assorted bandages. (Tennis players are always injured *somewhere*—have you noticed?) I'd been a member of my college team, played the tournament circuit for a time, and was truly hooked on the game, so when a friend said he could get me a membership at the famous Queen's Club, I hastily agreed. But then came the snag. How was I going to play when I could barely walk without suffering agony? And here my singing teacher came to the rescue. Yes, he was really supposed to be paying attention to my other end, but a man as brilliant as Maestro Georges Cunelli, teacher of Caruso, Laurence Olivier, Rex Harrison, and many other greats of the opera and theater world, was surely entitled to diversify a little. Anyway, he understood my craving to play tennis and actually encouraged me in this ambition. As a practical contribution he suggested I visit an unusual pair of German ladies who conducted classes in exercises specifically tailored for orthopedic problems. I went to see them and, after hearing my history and putting me through a few simple tests, they offered to give me one hour a day of exercises and deep massage under infra-red heat. They did no manipulation, only back massage, and I couldn't see how they could possibly make my condition worse. So I started these exercises in July, 1953.

By late August my back felt stronger and the pain was

less severe—somewhat easier to live with. However, the ladies advised me not to play tennis until all the pain had completely disappeared, which they estimated would take about six months.

I continued with them until the six-month period had elapsed and then, absolutely convinced that exercise and massage was the right approach, but not equally sure that these ladies knew the right exercises for my particular problem, I stopped the treatment.

During this period I had been hanging around the Queen's Club, watching matches and talking to the tournament players who practiced there, and I discovered that most of them suffered from back trouble to one degree or another. Lou Hoad, for instance, has a slipped disc and his pain is so severe that he was forced to give up tournament play for a long time.

One of England's leading players told me about a physiotherapist whom many of the players used for all sorts of orthopedic problems—backs, tennis elbows, knees, wrists, etc. He highly recommended this man and I reasoned that if he was good enough for top, world-class players, for a bum like me he'd be a Messiah. So I called and made an appointment to see him.

I found John K. to have a great deal of charm, a sympathetic ear, and a most refreshing approach to back problems. One, he did not believe in surgery for slipped discs, except as a last resort if the patient was so crippled and unable to get about that he had nothing to lose.

Two, he believed that the patient must help himself and that all the physiotherapist should do was show him how to develop powerful back muscles which would keep in place the jellylike substance within the disc and prevent the disc from slipping out of alignment and pressing on the sciatic nerve. He stressed over and over again that the solution to back problems lies in home exercise done religiously by the patient. I asked him how long it would take before I would be playing tennis again and he said if I did the exercises conscientiously for twenty minutes every morning and every evening, he estimated I should be playing gently within six months and as hard as I was able within the year. With this optimistic target in view, I enthusiastically agreed to work with him and we set an appointment for the next day.

I arrived at his office on Tuesday morning, December 22, 1953, and after the usual examination he showed me five exercises with which I was to begin. The first was one of the exercises the German ladies had given me, but the other four were completely different. He showed me how to do them properly, but when I attempted to do the new ones, I found I was totally unable. John explained that the muscles in my back were exceedingly weak both from the surgery and the lack of development. I wondered what I'd been doing for the last six months if not developing them, but at least I was on the right track now. I asked him about massage and he said he thought it beneficial, but only necessary when the muscles were in spasm and the patient was experiencing cramp pain. He suggested I buy exercise wall bars and have them set up in my house, as some of the exercises to come would involve hanging from this apparatus. Not by the neck, I hasten to say.

I tried again and again to do all the exercises John had shown me, but found most of them impossible. He massaged my back to relieve the muscle spasms and after forty-five minutes of this I felt like a man with a new back. He suggested I try the exercises next day and every day, and see him again in a week.

I awoke the next morning with bursting enthusiasm to take my first step along the road to the tennis courts, and dropped to my knees to begin the exercises. John had supplied me with a kind of shorthand sketch of them and, placing it in front of me, I launched into number one. My instructions were to do each exercise no more than five times until I was told to increase the number. John said it would take me about ten minutes to do them all and when I had finished I was to take a very hot bath. So far so good.

I had wall bars installed and as the weeks passed John added more exercises and increased the number of each to ten. My original enthusiasm had by now been lost in hard work and sweat, but my back really felt better than I had remembered it feeling for a long, long time. I kept up the exercises conscientiously, not missing one morning or one evening. The time it took to do them was by now running about twenty minutes and I was doing the full spate of them, numbering about ten in all. Two months had passed and I was now performing the exercises with great ease, which proved that my back had strengthened appreciably. I also had absolutely no pain at all except for an occasional dull ache when I became overtired. I started to pat the tennis-court canvas each time I walked by!

Five months and two days after I started my daily exercises, John suggested that I might hit a few balls with him at the Queen's Club. I was as excited as a kid on a first date as we dressed for my first tennis in well over two years. Just as well I wasn't on my first date since I had to wear a kind of corset brace, which John had prescribed for me. It sure wasn't romantic but it held my back firmly as I made that long-awaited walk onto the court. John turned out to be an excellent player and kept the ball in gentle play for about fifteen minutes. I found I had no trouble in moving freely and, although I tired rather quickly, I felt no pain or discomfort at all. We walked to the showers and he said he thought my movements showed no effects of undue adhesions from the surgery or muscle spasm from the exercise. He suggested I take a hot bath and he give me a massage.

He also said I could play gently, as we'd done that day, three times a week and as the months passed, we would build slowly to more violent tennis and longer sessions. He warned me again to continue the morning and evening exercises but excused me from the evening session on the days I played tennis. I scrupulously adhered to this routine and was thrilled to be once again on a tennis court, even though I was only volleying gently and for only fifteen minutes at a time.

The English climate was not helping my recovery and my back really felt the damp and cold, giving me an occasional bad day of back pain. However, the radiation down the leg had stopped completely and I was a thousand percent improved from those harrowing days prior to and immediately after my operation.

Twelve months after my first appointment with John, I played my first complete set of tennis. I was now running and hitting full out and not only was I playing, but now and then I was winning. I never played more than two sets or for longer than one hour (whichever came first) and I resisted all temptation to play more than three times a week.

At about this time I left the show and went to work in television and also about the same time John gave me permission to completely cut out the evening round of exercises. I was happy, fit, and enjoying life as much as

I had before that fatal night in *Finian's Rainbow*, and my wife at last uncrossed her fingers and stopped her eighteen hours a day of prayer.

And then, for no apparent reason, my back went into violent spasm. I was in extreme pain, unable to walk, stand, move, or even sit. It was pretty tough breathing, too. My wife called John, who ordered me to bed and arranged to visit me that evening at my home. To my amazement—and horror—upon arrival he told me to get out of bed and approach the wall bars. Frankly, the trip was a nightmare, but I had such faith in John that I eventually made it, with his help. Once there, holding on tight, I did a couple of very gentle hip rotations and movements which, to my surprise, hardly increased the pain at all. He then put me on all fours and made me do a few easy exercises, following them with a really deep, forty-five-minute massage. And after it I felt very much better.

What was interesting was that although the crippling pain had returned to my back, the radiating pain down my right leg had not returned. This, John explained, was proof that a disc had not slipped again and that the strengthened muscles were now doing their job. When I asked him what had caused the attack, he said the muscles had probably gone into spasm because of the extra work load from my strenuous tennis. He suggested that when I recovered I should once again go back to two exercise sessions a day for a while to additionally strengthen my back, and I reluctantly agreed. I seemed to have taken a big step backward.

Eight long, tedious weeks later, having interrupted the bed rest only to do the gentle exercises twice a day, I emerged from my prison and started work on a new musical film in which I was to star. I would believe that this film was a "sign" if I believed in "signs," because during the shooting I met an electrician called Tiny Roth, who had a back history pretty much like mine and who was now carrying around huge pieces of lighting equipment with no difficulty at all, and certainly with no pain or discomfort. I took to following Tiny around, inviting him to lunch, offering to pay his gambling debts —anything if he'd just put down the two-hundred-pound lamp he was toting around and tell me how he got cured. Finally, over a plateful of fish and chips in the studio cafeteria, he told me his story. He'd been in Libya on location when he was suddenly struck down with a spasm that locked him up as tight as a drum. Since he was in charge of the lighting, each day he missed was costing a fortune and the producers of the film were running around like crazy to find him a cure. Finally, Tiny never knew how, they unearthed a local folk doctor who had been unofficially treating parachute jumpers from Wheelus Air Force Base near Tripoli. Tiny was rushed along to see the man, Raschad A., and he swore that after doing Raschad's exercise program for several months, he had been totally cured.

"I'm still doing them same exercises," he said. "Every day."

"Sure," I said skeptically, "except for those occasional eight-week bed rests, huh?"

Tiny stared. "Bed rest? I've never had a day off work in ten years." He picked up the lamp and strolled off with it, while I tried to believe the unbelievable. Complete cure? Wow!

During the shooting, Tiny and I became good friends and I told him about my own exercises with John W., which made his lip curl.

"I know about that feller," he said. "An amatchoor. Raschad's a pro—'e starts where all the others leave orf. 'E's whatcher might call a specialist in backs. See?"

I saw. I also saw that those "signs" I didn't believe in were piling up thick on the ground, for only one week earlier I'd been invited by the British government to do a tour of the Middle East entertaining Her Majesty's troops. They were scattered around in Malta, Libya, Egypt, and Cyprus—that's right, Malta, *Libya*, Egypt, et cetera—and I suddenly stopped wondering how an American actor could say "no" to a queen. For now he didn't have to.

I had no idea if Raschad was still in business or even still alive, but there was no way I could talk myself out of making the effort to find him. My wife found a few ways, of course, like reminding me I was allergic to sand, flies, heat, Arabic, and bed sheets, but even she finally agreed it would be spitting in the eye of fate not to at least try. So in October, 1955, I left London for Malta, the first stop on my tour.

I could write a book about my trip to the Middle East —in fact, I *did* write a book about my trip to the Middle East *—but here I will confine myself to the happenings in Libya, which I hit around November 8. I settled into my hotel in Tripoli and asked the bell captain if he knew my man, Raschad. Without looking up from his racing form, he said, "Corfia," and held out his hand, which I gladly filled. What would the world be like without those guys?

Well, I borrowed a Jeep and made for Corfia, which was about ten miles from Wheelus. The roads there were unpaved mud, there were no signposts, no one spoke English, and my back was yelling murder. Finally I put it gently back into the Jeep and made for the base itself, where I had much better luck. After asking half a dozen U.S. airmen, all of whom spoke *some* English, I was introduced to a bunch of paratroopers who not only knew Raschad but were actually being treated by him. And with a beautifully drawn map in my hand, I again set out to find my Shangri-la.

* The Joker.

Raschad's office was a small room with no sign of the usual physiotherapy paraphernalia—diathermy machines, infra-red lamps, etc. In fact, the only things in the room were an examination table, exercise wall bars, a clean, well-padded mat, a clean, white-painted desk, and a clean, straight-backed chair with a clean brown gentleman seated upon it. He invited me to enter and I looked around, hesitated, and then cleaned off my shoes with a handkerchief. My wife should have seen that!

Well, I told Raschad who I was, who'd sent me, and how I'd managed to find him and he chuckled happily and offered me a seat—on the mat. I told him the history of my back and when I came to the part about surgery he clicked his tongue but didn't interrupt me. Then he told me to undress for examination and with deft, skillful fingers he examined my scar, tested the muscles in my back and legs, measured my reflexes and studied my posture and position while walking.

"You have a good scar—very few adhesions. You have excellent muscle tone and reflexes and almost no atrophy. You've been doing back exercises, yes?"

I told him about John and he nodded. "This gentleman has been prescribing the correct treatment for you. Why have you not remained his patient?"

"I had a bad relapse a while back and I felt—Tiny Roth felt—that you might be able to take me one step beyond John."

For some reason this statement sent Raschad into shrieks of delighted, infectious laughter, which he kept up so long that in spite of myself I was soon shrieking with him. When we'd both recovered our composure—me feeling very sheepish and Raschad muttering, "It is good to laugh," and dabbing at his eyes—he told me about his treatment. He said it was loosely based on the theory that man was not meant to stand erect and that we are all walking around with backs that are far too weak to support our weight in the upright position. As a result our muscles rebel and our vertebrae slip. He said what he attempts to do is to scientifically strengthen each and every back muscle, which must then take over the function of what should have been a much stronger and differently structured spinal column. He said his method involved taking Yoga, straining it through a fine mesh, adding a touch of old Libyan folk cure, a soupçon of Oriental wisdom . . . and then adding a hell of a lot of experience at treating crippled paratroopers from Wheelus. I laughed. Raschad didn't.

"How long will you remain in Libya?" he asked pleasantly.

"I'm here with a theatrical company. We're due to leave this area in about three weeks."

"Good, good," he said enthusiastically. "If we commence immediately and you work hard you will, in a very short time, know all I can teach you."

"How short?" I pressed.

"A week. Maybe two."

"Fine, Mr.—er—"

He sensed my predicament. "Please call me Raschad," he requested.

"I'm Jerry."

"Please, Jerry, shall we begin? Now the first thing you must remember is that it is you and your disciplined hard work which will eventually cure you completely. I am only the handmaiden to your work."

I smiled. Raschad didn't.

"I will teach you the exercises and make sure that you are doing them properly. The rest is up to you. As we progress I may discard some in favor of others, if I feel the need arises. It is also important that you approach your life-style with a calm and serene point of view. I know that in the West life is lived at a frantic and senseless pace. The tensions and hostilities we carry around with us are as much responsible for our aches and pains as anything else. You must understand that the main nerves of the body are carried in a huge electric wire coil down the spinal column, and when the brain transmits tensions and hostilities through these nerve fibers, the muscles that these nerves pass through are constantly being shocked and consequently react against this by going into spasm. It is this muscular spasm, or cramp, that causes most of the pain."

I was listening fascinated to this little man, who spoke slowly and quietly and with a great belief in his theory.

"In cases of accident, where there is an actual injury which shows clearly on an X ray, the cause is different—though still aggravated by tension—and therefore the treatment must be different. In the case of broken or chipped vertebra, a plaster cast must first be fitted so that the broken parts can heal. Then the muscles around these parts must be strengthened and now my treatment will again apply. In the case of muscle strains, or tears, the treatment is complete bed rest, with the afflicted parts immobilized by taping the back securely. In your case, however, we are dealing with a complex situation. You apparently had a slipped disc, which had you not been operated on, I would have been able to treat by strengthening the muscles of the back so tremendously that they would have pushed the disc back into proper alignment and thus relieved the pressure on the sciatic nerve. However, since you have had surgery, we have additional problems to solve. One, the disc itself has been removed. You have not had the vertebrae immediately above and below fused and therefore you are merely missing one vertebra. This, in itself, creates a back which is pathologically weak and, to add more trouble, the incision of the surgeon's knife has created scar tissue which itself presses on the nerves in that region and causes some pain. Also, because of the long history of pain, you have learned to compensate by moving your body while walking, standing, sitting, and even sleeping, into certain positions which ease the pain but set up new conditions which create new pain."

He stopped to see if I was with him, smiled, and continued.

"Therefore, our task is to rebuild your back muscles so that they will not only support your spinal column, weakened from the disc removal, but take over the function of the missing disc. We must teach you good posture at all times, even when sleeping, so that you break the vicious circle of pain, compensatory positioning of the body to relieve pain, causing more pain. Finally, and probably most important of all, we must try to impart to you a calm, carefree attitude toward life's values which eliminates tensions. This, in your highly industrialized world, will undoubtedly be difficult to sustain, but we shall try."

I sighed deeply as if to say, "All that in a week or two!" I was far from convinced but still anxious to give it a try. "Okay," I said. "You're the doctor, Doctor."

He again laughed, this time for ten minutes and, since "It is good to laugh," I joined in with him.

When we had recovered he said, "Right. To work. Please sit down on the floor and relax. Start from the top of your head and think of relaxing each small area, one at a time, until you have completely relaxed every muscle in your body. Start with the steel band around your head, think about that band and think about relaxing it. Then think of the muscles in your neck and relax them, wait until you have done so and then move downward, one muscle at a time until you have reached the tip of your toes. Do you think you can do that?"

I was so busy relaxing my neck I had difficulty in nodding, but I managed and continued the downward progress.

"Good! You may now tense up again," he said, giggling happily. "How do you feel?"

"Fine. Relaxed. Kind of tired."

"Good, good. That is how you should feel. Now we go to work."

"How long did I do this relaxing thing?"

"You were in a state of complete relaxation for about five minutes."

"It seemed like only a few seconds," I said, amazed. "Must I do this each time before I start?"

"It is good if you can," he said, smiling, "but the exercises will suffice. It is the exercises that put the body building blocks in correct alignment. So shall we begin?"

Thirty minutes later Raschad had put me through a basic eighteen exercises which he culled from his long list. Through trial and error he had found these to be most effective for general problems of backache. Out of the full eighteen only three were the same as John's and one like the German ladies'. I had therefore learned fourteen new exercises and my back felt great. Raschad then told me to dress and as I did he showed me a trick to use in walking, standing, and sitting to keep the "building blocks" properly aligned. Walk, stand and sit as if you had a string attached to the center of your breastplate and someone was pulling you forward by it. This causes the chest to be slightly pushed forward and the back slightly arched. When I tried it, I was amazed to discover how it did, in fact, keep the "blocks" in proper alignment. And I've been "on a string" ever since.

When I tried the exercises in my hotel that first day, I realized that they were very cleverly arranged in such a way as to involve the same muscles from the previous exercise in each subsequent one, and added on others as they progressed. I could tell this clearly by my new aches and pains, which were proof that those muscles now being used had long been idle. When I finished the routine I was huffing and puffing like a steam engine and my back was aching. But strangely, almost paradoxically, I felt a kind of strength even after one day's work, which made me walk more erectly and feel more secure. I fell asleep feeling that, contrary to the proverb, I *had* built Rome in a day.

I visited Raschad every day for ten days and became more and more impressed with the man, his simple philosophy of life, and his common-sense approach to orthopedic problems. Of course I knew I'd stand no chance at practicing a serene, relaxed existence on pressure-packed hermetically sealed Broadway, but I also knew I'd finally found a way of coping with my back that would allow me as busy, as active, and as pain-free a life as the next guy. And who could ask for more than that?

It is now nineteen years since I began to do the simple routine of exercises laid down by the two German ladies, John K., and Raschad. And to this day I have not had one attack, either serious or slight. I continually play violent tennis in competitive tournaments against boys twenty years my junior—and I have never experienced pain or discomfort. Occasionally I feel the pangs of hurt pride when I lose, but I never lose because my back's bothering me.

I may sound like one of those characters at an old-time prayer meeting who beg to be allowed to testify, but I want to testify to the fact that man *can* overcome one of the most debilitating and seemingly incurable problems of modern society. I did it, I feel great—and I am not alone. Thousands of people have discovered these exercises and taken a new lease on life—but the problem is still enormous.

Have you ever noticed that back sufferers make up about 75 percent of any crowd? Have you ever brought up the subject at a party? Sure, we all have. And what's the result? You hardly get started about your agony before you're nearly deafened by the other guests. Have they all got bad backs? You bet they have. If they're walking upright, that is. But they don't need to suffer any longer and neither do you, for these exercises *work*.

You must do the full series regularly, faithfully, and conscientiously. Once a day is sufficient unless you want to be an athlete, but no matter how often you do them, don't skimp, don't leave out a few, don't take it easy because you're hung over, late, broke, or about to be married. And another thing—don't tense up and immediately lie down when you have a backache. It may *feel* better lying down, but your back will *get* better if you do the most gentle of these exercises, namely Group I, Exercise 1, Group III, Exercise 3, (Parts 1 and 2), Group IV, Exercises 1 and 2. The pain will ease away in a very short time. Next day, or when you feel completely better, start the full daily routine. The muscles in your back will strengthen and the spasms will stop crippling you. Remember, you have absolutely nothing to lose.

Except your backache.

Exercises

THE following exercises are divided into five groups.

You begin with the easiest ones and build to the more difficult ones.

Group II is an extension of the exercises in Group I.

Group III is a further extension of Group II.

And so on.

You start with Group I.

Once your back has strengthened a little and your muscles are used to the added work load of the exercises, you will move on to Group II.

You must still, however, continue to do the exercises in Group I.

So that now you are doing Group I and Group II.

Then, when you are ready, you will move on to Group III.

Still doing Group I and Group II.

Try to think of these groups in the same way as you think of your back—as a series of building blocks. Group I is your foundation. Once you have learned the exercises in this group and are performing them effortlessly, you add to them the exercises in Group II, the second building block. When you are ready, and that means when you are doing all the exercises in the first two groups without undue strain or pain, then building block three—the exercises in Group III—can be added to your program.

Continue in this way until all five groups are included.

And you are doing the full series of exercises every day.

Easily and painlessly.

You will see that in most cases I suggest you start by doing a given exercise seven times and gradually increase to twenty times. You should do each exercise in Group I the full number of times before adding Group II to your schedule. Then do each exercise in Groups I and II the full number of times before adding Group III to your schedule, and so on.

You must do these exercises in the order given.

They are arranged to involve the same muscles from each previous exercise in each subsequent one, and new muscles are involved as the exercises progress.

In this way you proceed slowly and scientifically until you have fully involved all the muscles of the back which must be strengthened to relieve you of your pain.

You have placed the building blocks one on top of the other.

You will come to enjoy doing these exercises.

They are pain-relieving and body-toning.

They are of equal benefit to men and women.

You will feel generally better for them and, specifically, free of pain in your back.

And that is what we are after, after all.

Position A

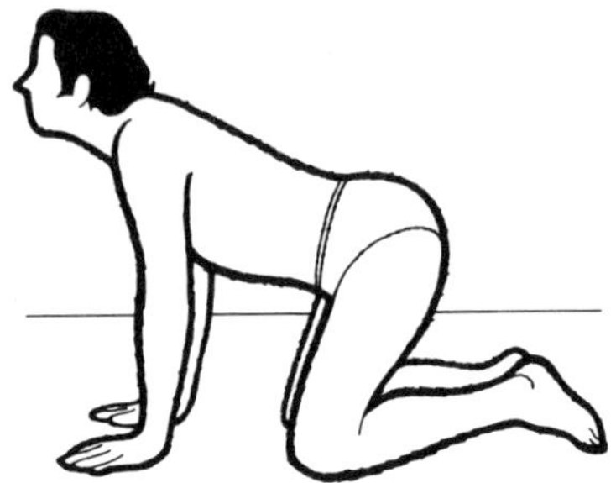

GET on all fours on the floor.
Keep knees and hands well apart.
Arch your back and lift up your chin as in Position A. Arch your back as much as you can. Lift your chin as high as you can.
Now raise your back and tuck in your chin as in Position B. Raise your back as high as you can. Tuck in your chin as close as you can.
Now combine A and B into one smooth exercise.
Do not pause between A and B.
Remember—do both parts of this exercise smoothly, not jerkily.
Start with seven and increase to twenty, adding one each day.

This exercise is designed to relax your lower-back

Position B

muscles and to relieve the spasm (cramp) which causes pain in the lower lumbar region.

By using contra-forces (first those that arch your back, then those that make it concave) you will work out the spasm.

This is what athletes do in their warming-up exercises to work out stiffness and aches from the previous day before they again involve their muscles in violent activity.

You will find that this exercise, alone, will ease tired backs and the minor aches and pains caused by bad posture. It will help you to stand erect without pain, even after a tough day.

Now for Exercise 2.

GROUP I: *Exercise 2*

Position A

SAME starting position as Exercise 1.

Move your left hip as far to the left as possible and at the same time turn your head to the left until you can see your left hip around your upper arm as in Position A.

Now move your right hip as far to the right as possible and at the same time turn your head to the right until you can see your right hip around your upper arm as in Position B.

Again—no pause between Position A and Position B.

Do this exercise smoothly and briskly.

Begin with seven and increase to twenty, adding one each day.

At first you may not be able to see your hip around

Position B

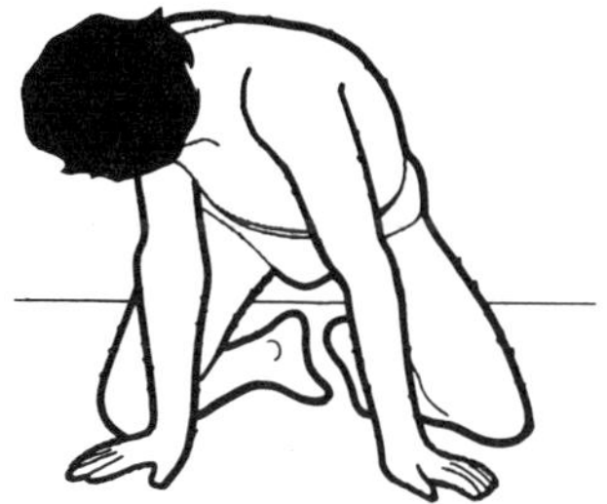

your upper arm but this exercise is designed to increase your suppleness and you will find that you soon can.

Suppleness is, of course, the opposite of stiffness.

And stiffness is the layman's term for tension.

When muscles contract and go into spasm, they are "in tension."

This exercise eliminates the tension in the hip and lower-back muscles.

You will feel a looseness and ease of movement as soon as you have done this exercise.

On to Exercise 3.

Position A

SAME starting position as Exercise 1.

Raise your right arm and reach for the ceiling as in Position A. Stretch your arm as far as you can.

Now lower your right arm and raise your left arm. Reach for the ceiling as in Position B. Stretch your left arm as far as you can.

Do not pause between Position A and Position B.

These two movements give you a count of one.

Start with seven and increase to twenty, adding one each day.

This exercise is designed to stretch the muscles in the middle and lower back.

By stretching these muscles, you ease away tension.

Position B

At the same time you are strengthening the very important muscles which help to support your lower back.

This concludes Group I.

You shouldn't need to limit yourself to the exercises in Group I for longer than the two weeks it takes to build to doing twenty of each, since they are basically exercises to relax existing tension.

However, if your back still feels a little tight, stay with Group I for a few more days.

Then proceed with Group II.

So far so good.

Right?

Onward!

GROUP II: *Exercise 1*

Position A

BEFORE starting the exercise, pick a spot on the wall directly behind you (a picture, a lamp, a doorknob, etc.).

Now face front, standing erect, legs spread comfortably, arms outstretched to the sides.

Keeping your arms outstretched, twist your body at the waist keeping hips and legs stationary.

First twist to the left until you can see the spot behind you as in Position A.

Then twist around completely to the right until you can again see the spot behind you as in Position B.

This gives you a count of one.

Make the movement from full around left to full around right continuous.

Do not break the exercise at the front position.

Position B

Twist smoothly and briskly.
Start with seven and increase to twenty, adding one each day.

This exercise involves movements which are made constantly in our day-to-day activity and usually made under stress.
It brings into play muscles which have become tense and painful due to this stress.
It relaxes and strengthens these lateral muscles which are located in the upper, middle, and lower back.
It generally tones up your back, allowing you to bend and turn without a single "Ouch!"
It's good for you!

Now on to Exercise 2.

Position A

STAND erect, legs spread comfortably.
Bend arms at the elbow and make fists.
Touch fists in front of you as in Position A.
Pull your elbows back as far as you can as though attempting to make them touch behind you, at the same time arching your back as in Position B.
Then return to starting Position A.
Do not stop at the starting position.
Make the back and forward movements continuous.
Do them smoothly and briskly.
Try to really make the muscles work—pretend your fists

Position B

are heavy and that your elbows are pulling the weight backward in the movement described.

Start with seven and increase to twenty, adding one each day.

This is an excellent relaxer for cramped upper-back muscles.

If at any time during the day you have been sitting in a cramped position too long, a few of these will bring immediate relief.

Now for the last exercise in Group II.

GROUP II: *Exercise 3*

Position A

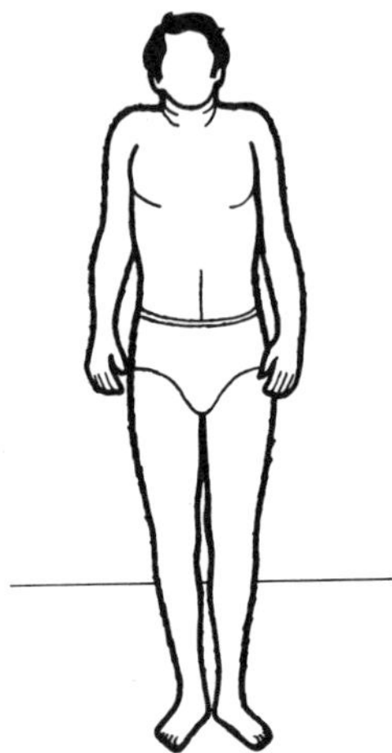

STAND erect, legs together, arms hanging loosely at sides.

Raise your shoulders as high as you can as in Position A.

Then lower them as low as you can as in Position B.

This gives you a count of one.

Do not stop in between raising and lowering your shoulders.

These two movements must be done as one continuous exercise, smoothly and briskly, like a pump.

Start with seventeen and increase to thirty, adding two each day.

This exercise relaxes and strengthens the shoulder and neck muscles.

Position B

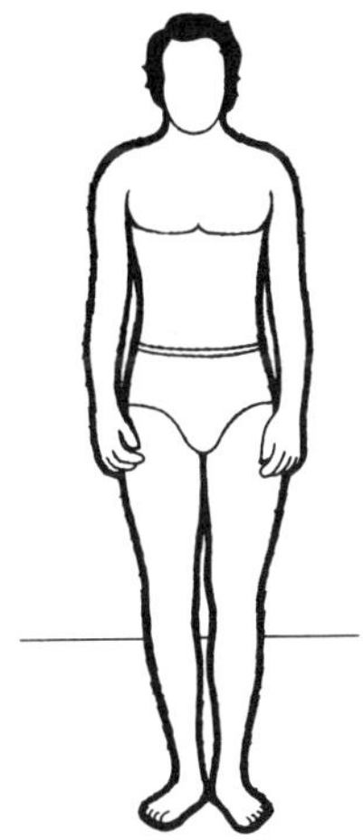

If you suffer from tension in the neck or pain in the shoulder joints, this is an excellent exercise for you.

It is also a must for us back sufferers, since pain in the shoulder and neck causes us to adopt compensatory posture which sets up tension in the closely related back muscles.

This concludes Group II.

As in Group I, two weeks should be long enough to build up to the full number of exercises in this group and to do them much more easily than when you started.

However, if you still feel a little stiff and insecure, stay with Groups I and II for another week.

After all, just think how long you've had your backache!

GROUP III: *Exercise 1, Part 1*

Position A

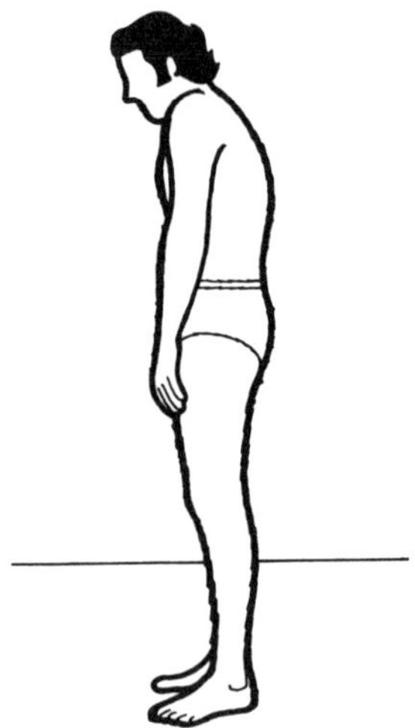

STAND erect, legs together, arms hanging loosely at sides.

Arch back and roll shoulders up and forward as in Position A, then down and back as in Position B, thus completing a circle.

Rotate the shoulders continuously, counting one each time you complete the circle and are back to the starting position.

Position B

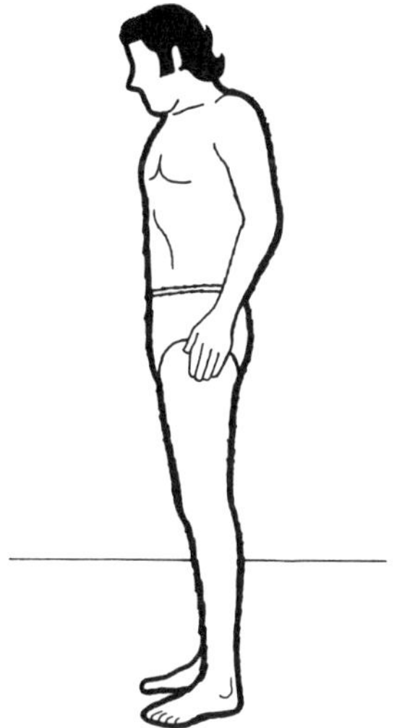

Do not stop between counts, so that by the count of ten (or thirty) you have really completed one long exercise.

Do this exercise smoothly and quickly.

Start with seventeen and increase to thirty, adding two each day.

Now do Part 2.

Position A

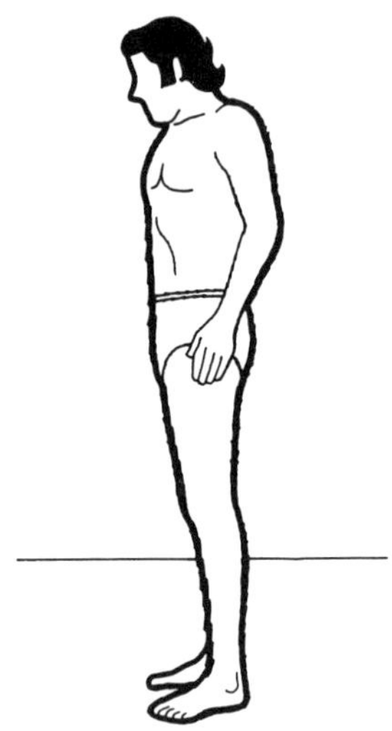

Now we will reverse the exercise.

Bring shoulders up and roll them back as in Position A, then down and forward as in Position B, thus completing a circle.

This is the same as in the first part of this exercise, but you are moving in the reverse direction.

As in Part 1, move smoothly and quickly.

Start with seventeen and increase to thirty, adding two each day.

This two-part exercise has the same effect as the last exercise in Group II.

Position B

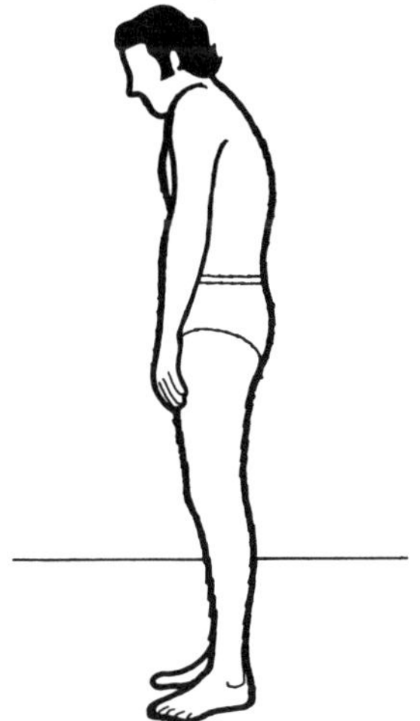

Only more so, because it builds on that exercise.
It is more vigorous and larger in scope.
It therefore makes the muscles of the shoulder and neck work harder.
And stretches and strengthens them still more.
It gives you a loose-limbed, tension-free feeling and does away with the chronic aches and pains that usually inhabit your upper back.
And who needs those?

Now—ready for Exercise 2?

Position A

STAND erect, legs together. Bend arms and hold elbows close to sides.

Keeping the trunk firm, twist the left hip forward and toward the right as in Position A.

Now twist the right hip forward and toward the left, as in Position B.

This gives you a count of one.

Do not stop between counts, so that by the count of ten (or thirty) you have really completed one long exercise.

Alternate these twisting movements, keeping them short and as fast as you can.

Remember the Twist? Like that—but fast and with legs stationary.

A gentle pumping motion with the arms helps to maintain good balance.

Position B

Start with seventeen and increase to thirty, adding two each day.

This exercise is designed to relax the lower-back muscles and help the hip joints move more easily.
It also yields an extra dividend. It helps to reduce your hips.
This is a good one to do during the day, for a few seconds, if you've been sittir g in one position too long.
It will provide immediate relief from muscle spasm.
Enjoy it!

Then move on to Exercise 3.

Position A

PLACE your hands, well spread, on a wall bar or the back of a chair at waist height. Grip the surface securely. Spread feet wide.

Rotate hips forward as in Position A, right as in B, and left as in C.

The movement is circular and continuous and resembles a stripteaser's grind.

Make as big a circle as you can.

Position B *Position C*

Do this exercise smoothly and make sure you feel pulling in your back muscles as well as your hip and thigh. You will only feel this pulling if the circle is big enough.

Do not do this one too quickly.

Start with seventeen and increase to thirty, adding two each day.

Now do Part 2.

Position A

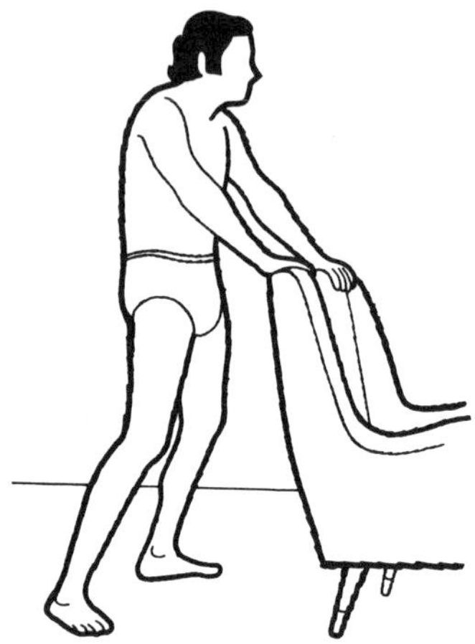

Now reverse the exercise.

Rotate hips forward as in Position A, left as in B, and right as in C.

This part of the exercise is done exactly as the previous part, except the circle is made in the opposite direction.

Start with seventeen and increase to thirty, adding two each day.

This two-part exercise relaxes and strengthens the lower-back and hip muscles.

Position B

Position C

It is a sure reliever for a tired and aching lower back and should be used whenever you feel a tightness developing.

A few of these at such times will help tremendously.

Congratulations!

You have now finished the exercises in Group III.

Continue to do them, as well as those from Group II and Group I, for about two weeks.

If you breeze through them easily, begin Group IV.

If not, continue doing Groups I, II, and III for one more week.

Then move on.

GROUP IV: *Exercise 1*

Position A

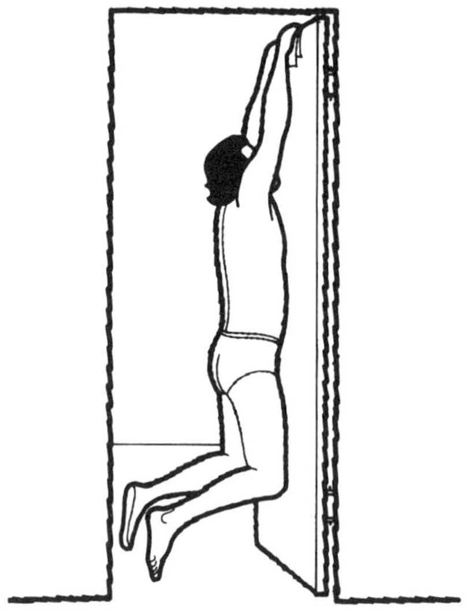

If you have wall bars, choose a rung high enough to allow your feet to hang clear of the floor.

If you do not have wall bars you can do this exercise just as effectively by hanging on the back of a door as in Position A. You will have to bend your knees, as you hang, so that your feet do not touch the floor. Put a towel over the top of the door so that the sharp edges will not cut into your hands. Make sure that the door is fully open and cannot swing while you hang.

Relax your body and hang free. Feel all the weight pulling on your lower back—not your arms. In other words, hang full out, making your weight deadweight. Do not pull up. This is an exercise for the back—not the arms and shoulders.

Hang like this for as long as you are able. Then get down and relax for about fifteen seconds.

Repeat this exercise three times. If you find you can increase to five the number of times you hang, so much the better.

This exercise provides natural traction.

Its purpose is to pull the vertebrae apart, thus relieving the pressure of the discs on the sciatic nerve. It also allows the discs to slip back into their correct position.

The discs are washerlike substances between the vertebrae which keep them from rubbing together.

It is the pressure of these discs on the sciatic nerve that causes the pain to radiate down your leg.

This exercise also helps keep the "building blocks" in proper alignment.

And also improves your posture which, in itself, helps eliminate back pain.

On to Exercise 2.

The following exercise is the first of the back extension exercises.

These exercises are designed solely to strengthen the muscles of the back.

At first you may have difficulty in holding your back in an arched position. That is because the muscles which hold your back in this position are weak.

This is proof enough that you need all the exercises in this book.

Do not be discouraged.

Do not give up.

You'll be amazed how quickly you will be doing these exercises easily.

Persevere!

And lose your backache.

GROUP IV: *Exercise 2*

Position A

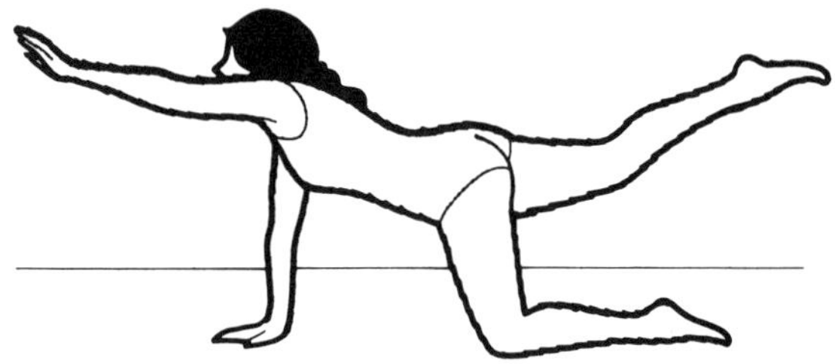

KNEEL on the floor on all fours. Spread your legs and keep arms apart so that you feel solid and comfortable.

Stretch your left arm and right leg out and up as far as you can, making your back as arched as possible.

Raise your chin so that your head follows the curve of your arched back as in Position A.

Hold for ten to fifteen seconds.

Return to starting position but do not pause.

Stretch your right arm and left leg out and up as far as you can, again making your back as arched as possible.

Position B

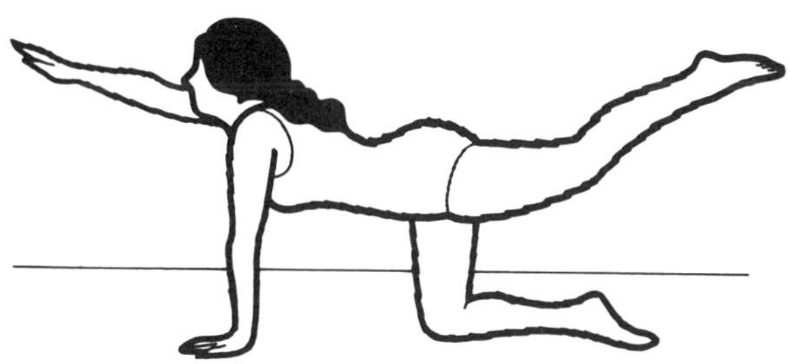

Raise your chin so that your head follows the curve of your arched back as in Position B.

Hold for ten to fifteen seconds.

Alternate these two movements, making one continuous exercise.

Count one after you have completed A and B.

Start with five and increase to ten, adding one each day.

Increase the time you hold each position to thirty seconds as your back strengthens.

Now do five of Exercise 1, Group I.

This is to completely relax the muscles and put the "building blocks" back into proper alignment.

You'll feel the results immediately.

Position A

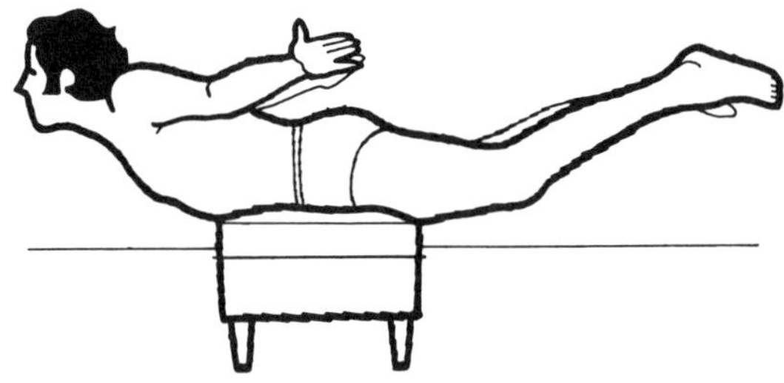

LIE, evenly balanced, over a low stool which should be positioned just under the pelvis.

Be sure the stool is sturdy and will not move.

The object of this exercise is to effect a maximum arch to your back using only your own muscles for support.

The optimal position is similar to a swan dive, but with legs apart.

So: in one smooth motion, extend arms sideways stretching outward and upward, tilt your head back and extend your legs outward and upward, keeping toes pointed as in Position A.

Do five of these, holding each for ten seconds. Increase holding time daily until you have reached thirty seconds for each.

When it starts to *hurt,* it is starting to do *good.*

The strain you feel is not harmful—it is strengthening your weak muscles.

As your back strengthens you will find the exercise progressively easier. And with a strong back, it's a cinch!

Well done!

You have now finished four groups of exercises.

If you are rarin' to go—start Group V immediately.

If not, once again repeat the first four groups for another week.

Then do Group V.

This last group is by far the most strenuous and by far the most efficacious.

Regardless of how difficult these exercises may seem the first time you do them, believe me, in no time at all you will be doing them like an old pro.

Easily and painlessly.

Keep at them.

They pay off.

Okay?

Let's go!

GROUP V: *Exercise 1, Part 1*

Position A

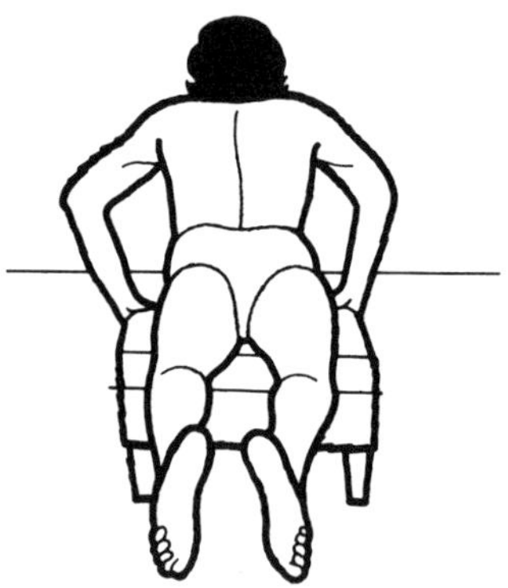

START as in the previous exercise (Group IV, Exercise 3, Position A).

Grasp the ends of the stool and push the trunk of your body upward, tilt your head back, and arch your back as much as you can.

Raise your legs as in Position A. Separate your legs as in Position B. Using these two positions, perform a

Position B

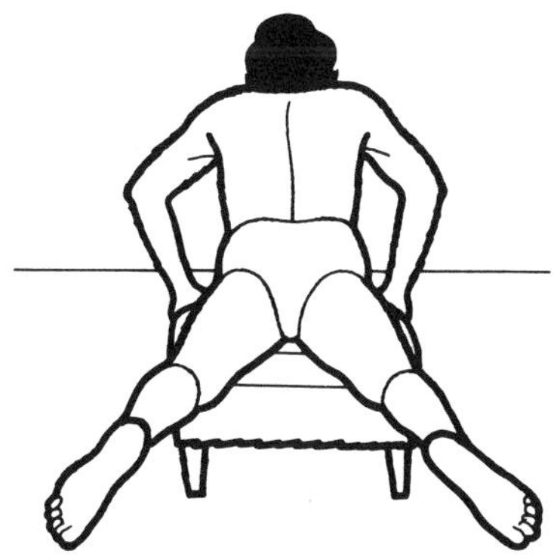

very fast, continuous, scissorlike motion.

Do these scissors fifteen times, increasing to thirty by adding two each day.

Fifteen scissors (or thirty) give you a count of one.

Five counts constitute this part of the exercise.

Rest for about ten seconds between each count.

Then do Part 2.

Position A

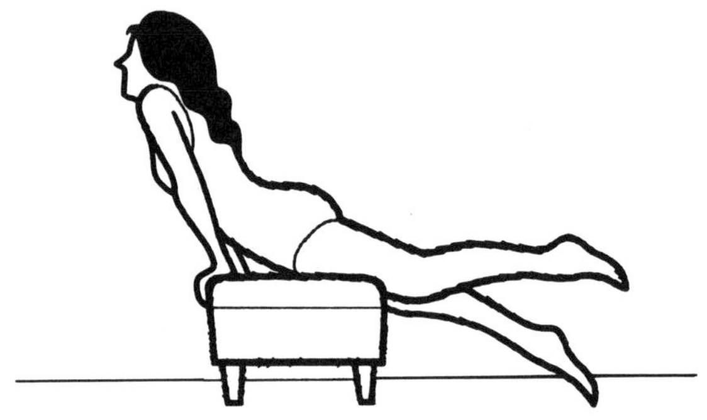

START as in Part 1 (Position A).

Grasp the ends of the stool and push the trunk of your body upward, tilt your head back, and arch your back as much as you can.

Keeping the legs stiff, move them rapidly up and down in short, fast bursts as in swimming (Position A).

Do these up-and-down bursts fifteen times, increasing to thirty by adding two each day.

Fifteen bursts (or thirty) give you a count of one.

Five counts constitute this part of the exercise.

Rest for about ten seconds between each count.

This two-part exercise is an extension of the previous one.

It adds extra stress on the muscles of the back by the movement of the legs and by pushing the trunk higher up into a more arched position.

It's easy to do and the effect on your back muscles is fantastic.

Again do five of Exercise 1, Group I, for relaxing the muscles. Feels great, doesn't it?

GROUP V: *Exercise 2*

Position A

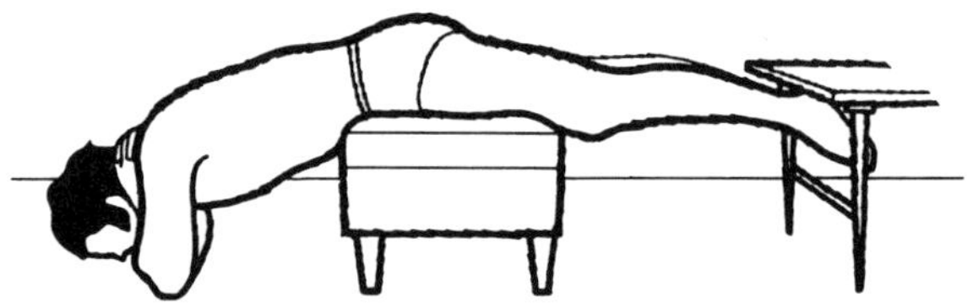

LIE over stool as in the previous exercise but move your body farther over the stool and hook your feet under an immovable desk, table, sofa, bed, etc. If none of these are available to hold your legs, another person can hold them for you, but you must be sure your legs do not move upward.

Make sure the stool is back far enough to give your trunk free sway to move up and down. You can tell if the stool is in the correct position if the entire strain is in the small of your back and it takes a

Position B

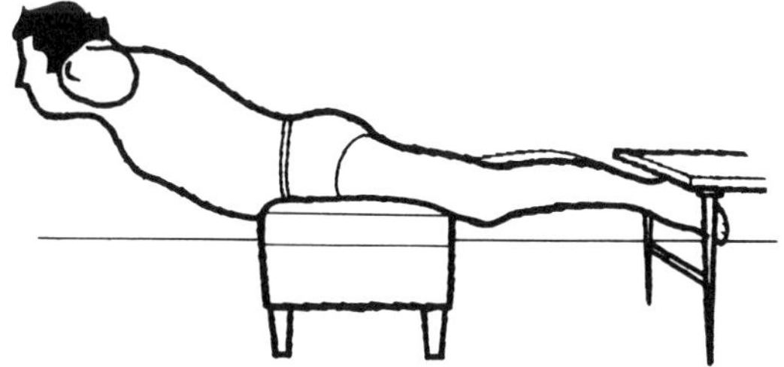

great effort to hold your back up into a high arch. If you can do this exercise without strain and effort, the stool is too far forward.

Now, with your head touching the floor, clasp your hands behind your head as in Position A. Raise your trunk up into a high arch. Tilt your head back and keep your hands clasped behind your neck as in Position B.

Hold for ten seconds, then lower your trunk and rest.

Do this exercise five times, increasing to ten by adding

one each week. Each week that you add one, try to increase the time you hold.

Eventually you will do ten and will be holding each for twenty seconds.

If, at first, the strain is too great, you can relieve it without stopping the exercise by retaining the back arch but unclasping your hands from behind your neck and reclasping them at the small of your back. Pull down with your hands and you will find the strain relieved.

As soon as you can, return hands behind neck, still not relaxing the back arch.

You may change the position of your hands to the small of your back several times during each count of the exercise.

This exercise is guaranteed to do the job.

It applies tremendous pressure on the back muscles and will give you a strong, powerful back that will hold the discs in place and relieve your backaches.

Don't be discouraged if it takes you a while to be able to do this one easily.

When I started I could barely raise my trunk an inch off the ground.

It wasn't long before I amazed myself by holding my back in a high arch for the full count.

Believe me, you will too.

Ready for the last one?

Go!

The final exercise is the pièce de resistance.

It is by far the most difficult exercise and it is not necessary for everyone to do it.

If you are a tennis player, a golfer, a baseball player; if you are involved in any active or violent sport, or if you hold a job which calls for heavy work—do it.

For you, it is essential.

If not, regard this one as the icing on the cake.

The previous exercises will do the job for you, strengthen your back, keep it strong and keep you free from pain.

But if you are able to do this exercise without too much strain—do it. It's good for you.

If it takes extra effort, keep at it.

If it is too much, leave it alone.

Position A

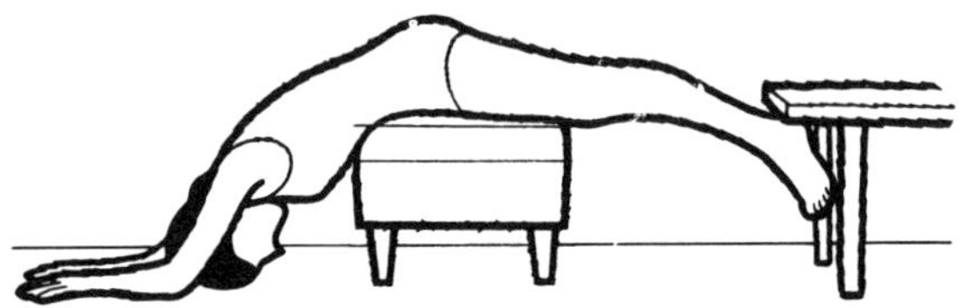

START as in the previous exercise (Group V, Exercise 2).

Extend your arms straight out in front of you on the floor as in Position A.

Now, keeping your arms stiff, raise your trunk and tilt your head back into a high arch as in Position B.

Hold for ten seconds, then lower your trunk and rest.

Do this exercise five times, increasing to ten by adding one each week. Each week that you add one, try to increase the time you hold.

Eventually you will do ten and will be holding each for twenty seconds.

If the strain is too great, relieve it as you did in the previous exercise, returning as soon as you can to the first position.

Position B

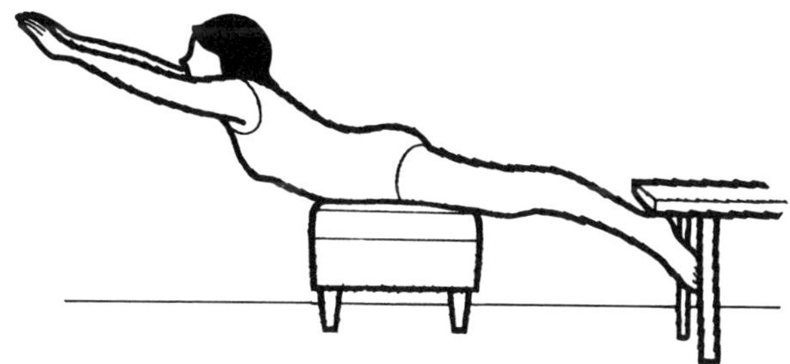

You may change the position of your hands several times during the exercise.

Do five more of Exercise 1, Group I.
Now take a hot bath and soak for ten minutes. If a bath is inconvenient, take a hot shower, concentrating the spray onto your back.

Remember, from here on in, you are the doctor.
You and you alone can cure yourself of your back pain.
Be diligent.
Be conscientious.
If you do these exercises correctly each and every day, with no days off for good behavior, I promise you that you will cure yourself of back pain and again enjoy life as you did before your back trouble started.

Do's and Don'ts

NEVER lift *anything* unnecessarily, no matter how light it may appear to be.

Under *no* condition should you lift anything *heavy*, (*i.e.* a heavy shopping bag, furniture, a suitcase, etc.).

If you cannot avoid lifting something *light*, lift it by bending your legs, keeping your back straight, firmly grasping the object, and then straightening your legs.

In other words, lift *only* with your legs, *never* with your back.

Do not make quick, jerky movements from the waist or hip. Do not move your trunk to the right, left, or rear while your legs face front. If you wish to turn,

turn your whole body in a smooth movement, keeping the building blocks one on top of the other.

In other words, move only in one direction at a time.

When your back begins to feel tired—rest.

If you cannot lie down on a hard surface (even the floor), sit down on a hard, straight-backed chair.

Do not slouch.

Walk as erectly as you can, remembering the trick about being pulled forward as if a string were attached to your breast plate, pulling you up and forward like a puppet on a string.

Do not watch long hours of television in a slouched, half-lying, half-sitting position. Either lie comfortably on a hard bed or sofa, properly supported by pillows under your neck and in the small of your back or, better yet, sit up straight in a good, firm chair.

At *all* times sleep on a hard mattress, either an orthopedic one or one with a board under it.

Never sleep in an air-conditioned room or with a draft blowing onto your back.

If you are sports-minded, get fitted by any good surgical appliance company for a surgical corset, but wear it *only* when you are participating in active sports.

If you need quick, temporary relief from pain, take two aspirin every three or four hours.

You should also buy an electric *fomentation* heating pad. These pads can be purchased at your drugstore or from the Battle Creek Equipment Company of Battle

Creek, Michigan. This company calls its product Thermophore. It is an on-off, moist heat which creates quick circulation of the blood in the painful area and relaxes the spasm causing the pain.

Do *not* use this pad *instead* of the exercises. It is merely a temporary, quick relief to get you going so that you can do your exercises free of pain.

Only the exercises can bring you permanent relief of your backaches.

Make them as much a part of your daily routine as brushing your teeth.

If you do these wonderful exercises religiously and over a long period, you will rid yourself once and for all of back pain, and will once again enjoy a normal life.

You're the doctor.

So prescribe these exercises for yourself regularly.

And here's to a happy and healthy new back!